A Little Guide
For Your Last Days

A Little Guide
For Your Last Days

by Jeffry Hendrix

Or

How You Too Can Grow to Like
My New Friend, Mort

Or

A Quick Read on How to Spend
Your Last Days/Weeks/Months
(Because a Little Time is All You've
Got)

Or

Advice on How to Face
The End of Your Life
From One Dying Beggar
to Another

What Others Are Saying

This little volume punches beyond its size. It's as huge as the question it asks - and as important. It is a memento mori. A reminder of death. It asks us to escape from the four walls of the self to the selfless freedom of the contemplation of the Four Last Things: Death, Judgement, Hell, and Heaven.

Paradoxically these Last Things are also the First Things. They are the first principles on which our lasting destiny, and our last destination, shall be decided. The first shall be last and the last shall be first ... We are Mortal. We will be Judged. And we will find our final resting place in either the Inferno or in Paradise. It's as simple and as scary as that!

Jeff Hendrix socks it to us like a Bible-thumping preacher, and yet does so with the sagacity of a latter day C.S. Lewis. Reading this little book is like going ten rounds with a pugilistic C.S. Lewis. It will knock you out and wake you up at the same time!

- Joseph Pearce,
   author, *C.S. Lewis and the Catholic Church*

Jeffry Hendrix's little handbook on dying well is a singularly clear-headed and consoling presentation of a subject we all avoid talking about. Most people in this world are distracted from their last end. In particular, those whose end is very near are often tempted to run to false securities. Hendrix's succeeds in focusing his readers on the things that really matter and does so by promoting what is really true, good and beautiful. He brings them to the heart of Christ through the 'chivalrous Marian virtue' of saying 'yes' to God.

- Fr. Angelo Mary Geiger,
Franciscan Friar of the Immaculate, author and speaker

Jeff Hendrix has written a pointed and poignant guide to dying well. Whether you have a terminal disease or not, you're going to face Mr Death. *A Little Guide for Your Last Days* is a moving, wise and witty way to prepare for the final adventure.

- Fr Dwight Longenecker,
author, *Praying the Rosary for Inner Healing*

Death is not something one gets right on the first try, and most of us put off thinking about it until our negligence is rudely interrupted by an sobering conversation with our physician. Jeff Hendrix has had such conversations, and he has written a wonderfully readable and wise and witty little book about what to do when that happens. Jeff takes death seriously, but his seriousness is suffused with an effervescent faith. A book about death that has a chapter entitled "Don't Swing at Every Pitch" is a book we all need to read.

- Gil Bailie,
author, *Violence Unveiled - Humanity at the Crossroads*

Copyright 2009 by **Jeffry Hendrix**

ISBN: 978-1-60104-024-4

Printed in the U.S.A.
Bridegroom Press

www.bridegroompress.com
E-mail: info@bridegroompress.com

Table of Contents

Introduction 5

Chapter One 11

Chapter Two 17

Chapter Three 27

Chapter Four 33

Chapter Five 37

Chapter Six 45

Chapter Seven 55

Chapter Eight 63

Chapter Nine 73

Chapter Ten 85

Acknowledgements 91

Introduction

When the Inevitable Becomes a Certainty

If you have been graced with the certainty of your own death due, perhaps, to a doctor's diagnosis of a terminal disease, you are already ahead of the great majority of human beings alive on earth. You know something from which millions upon millions of persons spend millions upon millions of dollars trying to distract themselves. In our day of militant, technologically-enhanced popular culture – and as never before in the history of the species *homo sapiens* – people want to keep as far as possible from the awareness of their own mortality.

It was only one hundred years ago that it was not at all unheard of for babies to be born in the home. So also, bodies were washed and prepared for burial there at times. And it was natural, since there was no alternative, for the elderly relatives to grow old, feeble, and die at home.

Today, all the above – birth, old age, death – are all kept rigorously (and profitably) far way from the consciousness of most persons. Want to make yourself a pariah of social opprobrium? Suggest that it be otherwise. No, the movies are filled with plenty of killing, sex, heartbreak of sickness, old age, and death – but they are all carefully, dutifully kept far away from the first person singular.

So, here you are! Raw reality has broken into your comfortable or uncomfortable personal space: There will come a time in the not so distant future when you and all your charms, characteristics, strengths, weaknesses, growing edges, and assets simply will not be here. Period.

Now, what is to be done with the time remaining to you? That's what this book is all about, my friend. Welcome to a very small, select club to which you would really rather not belong.

What I am here for is to convince you that (a) first of all, none of us can do otherwise, certain scientifically optimistic fellows to the contrary notwithstanding; and (b) you may as well take advantage of the opportunity to do what you really, truly want to do at the very core of your being. What might that be?

Before the end, I trust, you will know and be glad.

Chapter One

What Not To Do

The doctor has shrugged his/her shoulders. All that can be done has been done. It will be *x* number of weeks/months of relatively high functioning normalcy, a rather steeply descending slope toward the cessation of organ function, a call to Hospice, then a great deal of morphine or the like (you hope).

What should you do now? Let's start at the other end of the stick. What shouldn't you do? First of all, don't mimic any movie character, any television show plot line, any action of any saint, or any advice given to you by a well-wishing friend, relative, or acquaintance.

What about *The Bucket List*? You know, the movie with Jack and Morgan – the two old geezers who go about spending their money on fun and dangerous things? Sorry; that drops you right back to square one – distraction from awareness of your gifted knowledge. Do not under any circumstances fall for this ruse. At best, you will come out of the experience with that sinking realization that nothing has changed. At worst, you will provide the keepers of pop culture with yet another example of how to distract yourself to death. Literally.

Secondly, don't go round to acquaintances, friends, relatives, or perfect strangers looking for sympathy, understanding, concern, or anything else. Simply do not do it. They will not give it to you to the degree to which you are seeking. Even if they do, you will end up resenting their attempts. (Hey, they're "safe", or so they think. What's it costing them? Nothing.) Again, you will end up feeling worse than you did before you went looking for what they really and truly do not have to give to you.

In fact, once the fact is out there, you are in what some cultural anthropologists like René Girard call "the sacred precinct." You are a certifiable sacrificial victim, and you carry with you a sacred aura. Congratulations, right? It is an honor you would rather not enjoy, of course. As Mark Twain noted, when threatened by tarring and feathering and being ridden out of town on a rail, "If it weren't for the honor and glory of the thing, I'd just as soon walk."

And it isn't such a strange, metaphysical thing. Mortality, being so hidden and kept from the general awareness, makes death the thing of near-pornographic fascination today, as long as it is someone *else* who is being so fascinating.

So here is the advice: Don't waste your time in frenetic activities. It won't get you any closer to what you want the most. Neither will the most tender sympathies of friends, family, or perfect strangers. Nor will the bald awareness and contemplation of your status as being in the cattle chute, as it were. None of these will answer the question burning in your mind and heart. And what might that question be? The Big Question?

I think you already have some idea or you wouldn't have picked this book up from a bookstore like this. Matter of fact, you wouldn't have even come into this bookstore if you weren't already on the path to answering it for yourself.

Chapter Two

A Begging-Your-Pardon Personal Aside

To answer the Big Question, I am going to have to resort to some autobiography. I don't think it will bore too awfully much. But that, of course, is up to you to decide. My path in life brought me to the same place that you find yourself occupying, so I hope you will grin and bear with me, a card-carrying member of the Pre-Death Club like yourself.

In college, I swung wildly from the chaste, Bible-believing, C. S. Lewis-reading Evangelical to the unchaste, New Age hedonist. Sometimes I lived the two simultaneously. I dropped the latter lifestyle (above) and made a living from preaching the former as a respectable man of the Protestant cut of cloth. I eventually was blessed in finding a soulmate with whom I have been married for over 30 years.

But being a Protestant clergyman never satisfied me. It did not answer my biggest questions. I was fairly certain the Christian faith was true: We need a Savior from outside this world of time and space eventualities and social mayhem that we call human culture on this spinning planet in the vastness of space. The Christian faith makes the truth claim that this is precisely what happened +/- two thousand years ago in what is called the Incarnation: We got a Savior.

I accepted this, affirmed it, cherished it. I give thanks for my Protestant Christian roots that taught it to me. But it didn't fill needs, didn't satisfy, didn't answer all the questions let alone the Big Question.

Even as a pastor - leading souls, blessing births, praying at bedsides, sending the dead on their way – I was not getting what I wanted, needed, at the core of my being. I tried contemplative prayer in an ecumenical book study led by two monks from a nearby Catholic monastery. I entered Jungian therapy, a Jungian book study, the C. G. Jung Society of my area. I attended fantastic folk music concerts. I was a David Letterman junkie. I was your basic left-leaning New Age Zen Protestant pastor who believed in Jesus Christ "as my personal Lord and Savior," as they say. But it never got me near to answering the Big Question.

This went on for years... no, decades. Eventually, however, I noticed something. All the best answers I was receiving were coming from one particular sector of the known galaxy of influences on my life. These answers, though piecemeal – as befitting my eclectic, scattered approach to life – were coming from persons affiliated with the Catholic Church.

Thomas Merton. J. R. R. Tolkien. Dorothy Day. Walker Percy. G. K. Chesterton. Later, Ronald Knox. René Girard. Gil Bailie. Joseph

Pearce (and all of his *Literary Converts*). And, once the sluice was fully opened, more and more and more.

Unlike members of my family one generation before me, I did not hold an onus against the Catholic Church. I didn't reject it out of hand from all of the influences in my life. You may have noticed that about me in the sentence about attending an ecumenical book study at an abbey. Indeed, I made what Catholics call a *retreat* nearly every year during all of my pastoring years at the same abbey where the book study took place.

And there it was that I made an astonishing discovery. I, who was already convinced that Jesus Is the Way, began to have what Cardinal Newman called sufficient "illative" proof that the Catholic Church was, is, and ever will be the Church Our Lord founded on Saint Peter ("Rocky"), and about which He promised "the gates of hell shall not prevail against it" (*Mt 16:18*). Or, at least I was willing to presuppose it and go looking to see if I could prove otherwise.

I won't go into that search here, it isn't the reason for this book and I am not an apologist. For that matter, I am not a spiritual director either. And that may tell you something about the nature of the Big Question if you still paying attention and trying to see if I have anything to help you in your newly acquired position of finding that you belong to the Pre-Death Club.

So I converted. I entered into full communion with the Catholic Church. Swam the Tiber. Poped. Early on, I'd say that I felt like a fulfilled Protestant, but too many Protestants took umbrage at that, so I stopped out of charity (though it was true).

The long and short of it is – and here's your opportunity to close the book and put it back on the shelf – entering the Catholic Church was the most grace-filled decision I have ever made. Now, if you do stop here, please *do* put the book back, don't heave it across the room, tear it page from page, or otherwise damage it. (If you go through a buffet you don't spit on the food you don't like, do you? You *do*? Well, you shouldn't.)

But if you continue to read now, knowing full well that I am a Catholic convert, am happy about it, and am certain that it was the most important decision I have ever made, then I will go ahead and tell you what the Big Question is. It has two parts. Ready?

The Big Question is this: **Why am I still here, and what am I supposed to do with the time I still have left?**

Now that I've said it, you knew it already, didn't you? That is just fine. As I said before, you would not have picked this book up, let alone come into this bookstore if you hadn't been most of the way to asking it yourself already. This is the great thing about Socrates and what the Church Fathers saw about him: The Socratic method presupposes that there is a knowledge in you that only needs a question to dislodge it into a fuller awareness.

What the Christian faith says, however, is that this knowledge is not just a goal attainable to a favored few – a secret gnosis guarded for a select few *illuminati* – but rather something at the heart of every person ever born. It is a portion of what is called being made in God's image, *imago dei*. And that is where, ultimately, we will find the answer to the Big Question.

Chapter Three

*What's God's Love
Got to Do with It?*

EVERYTHING

Earlier we spoke of Our Lord founding His Church upon Saint Peter. In John 6, Jesus asks the disciples, "Do you also want to leave (me)?" Peter replies, ""Master, to whom shall we go? You have the words of eternal life. We have come to believe and are convinced that you are the Holy One of God" (*69*).

If you can think of any other source of grace, strength, hope, faith, or love than Our Lord, then, once again, close this book and walk away from it. Good luck to you with that. I will here on presuppose that God Incarnate, the Word made flesh (*Jn 1:14*) is the conduit of God's grace for our lives, and that there is nothing that can separate us from His love. Nothing can separate us from His love so long as we stay in a faith relationship with Him through the Church He Himself founded and sustains with His Holy Spirit in history.

From Our Lord himself, one need not look any farther than Luke 12, 4: *"I tell you, my friends,* **do not fear those who kill the body,** *and after that have no more that they can do"* (emphasis added). I must understand Our Lord to mean that we should not fear not only people who can take life, but other agents of destruction; like hurricanes, floods, cancer, bacteria, raging bulls, and train wrecks, plummeting F-18s, to name a few.

One may not be pleased at the onset of pain – who in the world is? Our Lord Himself felt the anguish of it in the Garden of Gethsemane (*Mt 26:36ff; Mk 14:32ff; Lk 22:39ff; Jn 18:1ff*), proof that He was truly one-with us in the flesh. We have in Him, as *Hebrews* reminds us, "a great high priest who has passed through the heavens, Jesus, the Son of God, let us hold fast to our confession. For we do not have a high priest who is unable to *sympathize with our weaknesses*, but one *who has similarly been tested in every way*, yet without sin" (4, 14-15, emphases added).

Okay, so once we have established that we have The Man in our corner, we face the prospect of imminent death differently than those bereft of this consolation. But hold on. Wait a moment. How do we *KNOW* He is in "our corner?"

Part of knowing this for certain comes directly from Jesus Himself. There are many misperceptions about the nature of God – from seeing Him as a Taskmaster who treats us like slaves (Islam); to a warm, mushy deity who only expects us to be "nice people" and ushers into Heaven all manner of riff raff (New Age Salvation Lite); to a stern, all-demanding Judge who divides humanity into (a) the "elect", who automatically have an "get out of jail – go directly to Heaven" card and (b) the damned, who are pre-ordained to go to "h-e-double-hockey-sticks" – too bad for them (Classical Protestantism).

But Jesus in the Gospels makes it exceptionally clear as to the nature of God with whom He is part and parcel.

God makes it manifestly clear that (a) He does the deciding; *we* are not to judge, "lest we be judged;" (b) He is just like the Father in the parable of the Prodigal Son (*Lk 15:11ff*), willing even to look foolish on behalf of the one who sheepishly returns to the ranch from a life of sin, looking for work, room and board; and (c) He is willing to go so far as to die an ignominious and wrenchingly-painful death – death on a cross – for the sake of a bloodthirsty and largely thankless human race.

If that is not love, what is? We need to hurry it along.

Chapter Four

A Breather

A Brief Look at Club Membership

This is a short chapter, a breather, if you will, and recap of the Introduction (above). If you know you're on the short list for the oldest and least appreciated friend of the human race – *Mort* – then your chances of dying well are enhanced exponentially. The basis for this is built on the nature of mortals (that's us) and the source of our being - our *ontology*, philosophers call it - who shares *being* with us in the first place (that's God). If we are deluded about either of these realities, our chances of dying well - do what we will or will not - are nil.

So! *Are* you good to go, as they say? No? Not yet? Okay. Not to worry. The next few chapters (time is short and precious) are the how-to section of this book. You will, of course, tailor them to your situation and time limits. So let's just say for the sake of time that you want to "practice" being an angel right now. Well, sorry. It's not possible (or good theology), but it shows that you are being drawn by the Father just as Our Lord said:

> *"No one can **come** to me unless the **Father** who sent me **draw** him, and **I** will raise him on the last day." (Jn 6:44, emphases added)*

You are leaning toward faith, hope, and love like the man who brought his son to Jesus for healing and said, "Lord, I believe; help my unbelief!" (*Mk 9:24*). Your "disordered passions" are being re-aligned with the will of God, and the Holy Spirit is moving you by grace heavenward in sanctification. How cool is that, as the kids say?

Even the mistakes you make can help you farther down the road. I trust you. "Offer it up" and you'll do just fine. Let's dive in. The water is fine.

Chapter Five

Retreat

Have you been to a monastery on retreat? Lived, even for a weekend, in the rhythm of the Liturgy of the Hours, prayed in the quiet of the abbey chapel, eaten the simple fare of a convent guesthouse?

I won't wax poetic about it. I simply recommend that you find a Catholic monastic setting near you, make a reservation, and go on retreat. Going on retreat removes you from the normal bustle of your worldly routine, and, if your illness has not robbed you of it yet, it is good practice for what will inevitably happen anyway.

This way, you are practicing being out of control of your schedule and willingly trying to take part in a way of living and praying that has been an active alternative to the world since Saint Benedict started the monastic ball rolling in the fifth century.

I prefer a silent retreat that relies on the actual offices of the monks to give it form and substance. Each day of the retreat, this way, is an effort in aligning one's living and praying with that of the monastic community. And why is this important? Well, if you hadn't thought about it yet, *who* do you think is going to need to do the bending and adjusting to get used to Heaven – the vast multitude of angelic beings all enjoying the Beatific Vision? Or *you*? If you said the latter – good. If you said the former, you still have quite a reality check ahead of you. As C. S. Lewis said, Heaven is an acquired taste.

But time is short now. I strongly recommend that while you are on your retreat, you spend as much time as possible before the Blessed Sacrament in the Tabernacle praying for your loved ones. This is your chance!

The Real Presence of Jesus is one of the greatest reasons for my conversion. Go to Him, sit with Him, kneel before Him. But most of all, take your family, loved ones, friends and enemies before Him and commend them to the care of our Good Shepherd. Pray that they will increasingly hear His Voice, and answer Him when He calls them.

A great aspect of a retreat is that nearly all guesthouses make time available for retreatants to meet with a priest, either for spiritual direction, the Sacrament of Reconciliation, or both. Take advantage of this important opportunity!

Many guesthouses are also blessed to have excellent libraries that retreatants may – if allowed – borrow from to take books back to their rooms. In my experience, just visiting the quiet of the guesthouse library and allowing your eyes to range over the titles can bring wonderful events of serendipity of the Holy Spirit to your life.

And, monastic settings being what they are, there are usually spacious grounds to stroll, allowing one's heart to turn to the Author of all you see.

> *"Are not five sparrows sold for two small coins?*
> *Yet not one of them has escaped the notice of God.*
> *Even the hairs of your head have all been count-*
> *ed. Do not be afraid. You are worth more than*
> *many sparrows." (Jesus in Lk 12:6-7)*

+ + +

A retreat in a monastic setting, complete with Sacrament of Reconciliation, centered on the rhythm of the Hours, prayer for family and loved ones before the Tabernacle, receiving the Holy Eucharist, is a fantastic way to reorient your life and your impending death to the glory of the One Who made you, gave you life, sustained you, redeemed you, and will sanctify you all the way to Heaven.

Chapter Six

Don't Swing at Every Pitch

S o what pitches should you swing at? First, as far as is humanly possible, show your love for your family by not bequeathing to them outstanding debts. This is not always possible, medical expenses being what they are. But you should use every means available to you not to leave them in the lurch financially speaking.

You can't avoid it? While you have the energy, use it: Call a reputable consumer credit counseling organization that will help consolidate your bills and, we both hope, will help make debts manageable when you are gone. As unpalatable a task as it seems, this will be one of the greatest gifts you can pass along to your loved ones.

If you aren't indebted financially, give to the best causes that need your gifts *NOW*. Don't wait. Enjoy seeing your resources go to worthy organizations, the greatest one being your Diocese or local parish church and/or school. Parochial schools in America are feeling the effects of ageing just like so many societal infrastructures. Buildings, windows, and h/vac systems are old and in need of repair or replacement. Catholic schools offer the finest education in the land, but struggle to keep up with the need for evernewer technologies. Earmark them in your will or through an endowment. And don't forget a great tradition: Set aside some money for Masses to be said for the repose of your loved ones' souls (and *yours*).

So much for finances. Get it done as quickly as possible and behind you, if possible. Let's move on to what may be the most difficult aspects of belonging to the Pre-Death Club.

These will be tough times for you emotionally and spiritually, but not necessarily without dividends in both areas. My first recommendation here is to call the parish office, make an appointment with a priest of your choice for the opportunity of sharing what is going on with you.

He will really want to know, and will want updates. Make frequent use of the Sacrament of Reconciliation; it is just common sense for you to remain in a state of grace. Why? Besides the obvious reason of assuring a close relationship with the Most Blessed Trinity (as close as is possible here on earth), you will also be putting yourself in position to receive and be aware of more emotional and spiritual benefits coming your way during your last days here.

God is constantly sending us reassurances, private revelations, consolations, and blessings. Did you know that? The trouble is, our "antennae" are often either pointed in the wrong direction and don't even pick them up, or we're so self-absorbed – not being in a state of grace

– that we want something *else*, and our hands are not open to receive what God knows is good for us.

Make it a primary goal to receive the Sacrifice of the Mass every Sunday or more often – out of self-interest if you cannot rise to doing it out of love of God. Receive Our Lord, body, blood, soul, and divinity, in this Blessed Sacrament, the "Source and summit" of the Church.

Another vital Sacrament instituted by Our Lord, though often forgotten today, is the Anointing of the Sick. Just as you need to keep your priest apprised of your condition, you *will* want to receive this sacrament. The priest who administers it can also impart the apostolic blessing with its attached plenary indulgence. Suffice it to say, a plenary indulgence is of great importance on your way to Heaven. Ask your priest about indulgences – your time now is precious. In this way, Anointing of the Sick is the supreme Sacrament to prepare you for your Final Journey. Celebrated with Holy Communion – your Bread for the journey, *"viaticum"* - and received by you within the state of grace – r*emember* how important that is! - it will be your ultimate preparation and "offering up."

> *The Anointing of the Sick completes our conformity to the death and Resurrection of Christ, just as Baptism began it ... This last anointing fortifies the end of our earthly life like a solid rampart for the final struggles before entering the Father's house (Council of Trent, quoted in the Catechism of the Catholic Church, No. 1523).*

And while I'm speaking of the emotional and spiritual, here is an important caution. You will be tempted to many, many false conversions throughout your last days. Count on it.

These are "pitches" you most assuredly do *not* want to swing at. I mentioned them back in the

Chapter One. They include mimicking movie characters, chasing after quack cures with a false hope in something other than the Christian faith, becoming a "*human doing*" rather than a human being in an effort to distract you from the reality of your mortality. It will only make things worse if you do any of these inauthentic distractions.

You stuck with me this far, stick a little longer. I am going to say something you don't want to hear, but you need to. And here it is: You will fail. You *will* fall flat on your face chasing distractions. You'll wake up and say something like, "Oh no. *Not again.*"

But here is what you will do: Go to Confession, again. Just tell it, and listen to the words your Confessor tells you. Then you will grasp the grace that God gives you to see that temptation coming and you will avoid it the next time.

Will it happen again? Sigh. Sin is sneaky. It likes to slip into a little different guise and present itself as something *totally new* – yeah, right.

For me, it came finally to saying internally, "All right. That's the last time I will *ever* have to confess that to a priest," and meaning it. Absolutely, totally, end of story.

But are there *some* distractions that are okay? I can hear your question from here. As long as you keep your condition in mind, have a ball! Eat, drink, and be merry – within limits. How long do you have left to smile, make someone else happy for a truly good reason, bless and be a blessing to others? Of course there are distractions that are just fine.

Humor – even gallows humor – is something even the saints engaged in. Like Saint Thomas More. Do you remember what he said to the headsman as he went to the block? "Be careful of my beard, it hath committed no treason." You may even help other persons come to grips with their mortality in a way that makes the Spirit's work of sanctification easier for them. Just be kind: Death is a heady draught.

Chapter Seven

Truth, Goodness, and Beauty

Okay, I promise. This won't be a chapter about cheap thrills at museums or schlock like that. In fact, I will tell you up front that it will consist of several examples of Truth, Goodness and Beauty from places like the movies so that if you want to you can skip this chapter altogether or come back later.

There was a time in the movie industry when scripts having to do with eternity were a hot commodity. In the 1920s and 30s, Americans knew what it was to say goodbye to a relative, even their own children, due to polio, the flu, and tuberculosis. I won't say that Hollywood rode the wave of premature death with the profit motive in mind, but I will say that they turned out some really good films dealing with death, angels, misfortune, and a belief in eternal life.

One of the best of these is *On Borrowed Time* (1939), with Lionel Barrymore, in which a grandfather has to deal with the death of his wife and grandson, "Pud." It spells out in no uncertain terms the inevitability of death and our need to submit to it with grace. Here is a short list of others that deal with the realities of life and death and a gracious, loving God (but there are, of course, more): *It's a Wonderful Life* (1946), *The Bishop's Wife* (1947), any version of Dicken's *Christmas Carol* (including Bill Murray's superb *Scrooged* and excluding the politically-correct 1999 version starring Patrick Stewart).

Do you have recollection of a piece of music that you found moving? Get it and listen to it. A book or series of books (like Tolkien's *Lord of the Rings*) that seemed brim full of a sense of hope and a reality beyond despair. Find them and reread them.

In other words, the Holy Spirit is unscrupulous in trying to infuse you with faith, hope, charity and all the virtues – even through such a medium as the movies. The only cautionary word I have is that you must remember there is a gradient of dumbing down in terms of how we are saved that goes from a gentle slope to a steep drop-off in the history of movie "magic." And as I said back in Chapter Three, the true nature of God is a forthright given; it isn't negotiable on our part, as though we could sit down and "hammer out" the terms of salvation somehow through collective bargaining.

For our part, we must abide by the teachings of Mother Church. Do your utmost to love God with all our heart, soul, mind, and strength; and our neighbor as our self. Remain in that state of sacramental grace granted by the Church, which was founded by Our Lord. Keep your priest up to date on your condition.

For God's part, well, God may extend His grace to whomever, as in the case of Saint Paul who was outside the Church when he got his summons on the road to Damascus (*Acts 9*). But we stray from it to our peril and in our pride. Time is short – best keep to the Way vouchsafed by the Magisterium of the Catholic Church. Period.

Anyway, the farther that the Holy Spirit brings you during this dying process in sanctification, the more your taste and awareness of truth, beauty, and goodness will grow. Why? Because God's grace is transforming you all the while. Saint Paul put it beautifully.

So we do not lose heart. Though our outer nature is wasting away, our inner nature is being renewed every day. For this slight momentary affliction is preparing us for an eternal weight of glory beyond all comparison, because we look not to the things that are seen but to the things that are unseen; for the things that are seen are transient, but the things that are unseen are eternal. – II Cor. 4:16-18

Once again I remind you of the obvious: You are dying and you know it. Your ability to decide how you will die – whether enjoying the fullness of God's grace through the sacramental life of the Catholic Church, or not – is up to you. If you choose the former, you can count on a deepening awareness of God's truth, goodness, and beauty. Let me turn quickly to three last chapters and a few things that you can truly look forward to, even here and now in what C. S. Lewis aptly called "the shadowlands."

Chapter Eight

Friendship

I said earlier in Chapter One that seeking out friends in an attempt to evoke sympathy, loving gestures, and concern is something you should *not* do. But that does not mean that friends are not to be sought out at all. By no means. The trick is, don't look to get answers to the Big Question – remember it?

Why am I still here, and what am I supposed to do with the time I still have?

Being the certified sacrificial victim awaiting execution of sentence that you are, they may or may not appreciate being in your presence. Find the distance at which they *are* comfortable – a phone call now and then, e-mail, texting, maybe if you are extremely blessed, an evening now and then for drinks and/or dinner. You will find and know the right distance.

And don't hold it against them if you find they struggle with their ambiguous feelings toward you. They *can't* give you want you want the most. We are going forward in this program of Pre-Death Club membership with a working assumption that Our Lord was not fooling around when He said this in the canonical Scriptures:

> "... *seek first HIS KINGDOM and His righteousness, and all these things shall be yours as well*" (Mtt 6:33, emphasis added).

If your physician – surgeon, oncologist, whomever – has befriended you, this goes for him or her as well. You simply must remember that medical sciences are still only a step away from the natives throwing herbs and flower garlands into the volcano, regardless of the cool, non-existent gadgets that Dr. Beverly Crusher waves over her patients and cures with in *Star Trek – The Next Generation*. Doctors need to maintain a certain distance for the sake of objectivity and professionalism, not to mention their sanity. When the shrug comes, believe them. And do not – *do not* – forget to thank them for everything they did. Promise?

But there will be great friendship through out your tenure in the Club if you are willing to realize that gold is where you find it. You can't be picky. The Holy Spirit will assuredly send you help, assurance, comfort, and consolation in strange packages and at funny times when least expected. Get used to it, my friend. Remember: *You* are the one who needs to adjust to Heaven, not the other way around.

But the one who you need to remember to keep close to you is, once again, your Confessor. In Dantean terms, he holds not only the Gold key to bind and loose from Our Lord Himself (!), but also the Silver key of soul friendship. If you allow him.

And one final word on friends and family: I had to offer you a warning on expectations. What to you may only be a natural desire to be close *in extremis* can all too often be read as "neediness" or "clinginess" by those who, when everyone is well and brimming with life, would find you a hale fellow well met.

So by all means keep folk up on how you are: your modeling for them how to do it may, in fact, when they (finally) come to the point on their inevitable journey toward death, be a huge grace for them. It is a fine thing to show others how to die with faith, hope, and charity, to the best of our ability.

Having said that, you are now in the "sacred precinct" of the sacrificial victim, anthropologically speaking. And as Andrew McKenna notes such persons are afforded what he calls the "victim's epistemological privilege." That is, you see things more clearly than you ever have all of your life. So, going back to the emotional and spiritual matters I talked about in Chapter Six, don't hold it against others for not seeing things as you see them.

Resentment is a real danger here. It can interfere with getting what you really and truly want, the answer to the Big Question and many other things besides. And, if you are not careful, it will blind you to those graces and friendships that the Holy Spirit *does* send your way. So let me offer a strategy, a technique, that you may accept or reject.

A prayer that I have found as a spiritual "tool" of immense help is what the Eastern Church calls The Jesus Prayer. Its origin is in the words of a man in Our Lord's parable in Luke 18,13: "God, be merciful to me, a sinner!" The actual Jesus Prayer is:

> *Lord Jesus Christ, Son of God, have mercy on me, a sinner.*

Short, easy to memorize, trips off the tongue, even at three a.m. in the morning or in a hospital setting. Now, here is my recommendation. After crossing yourself – the timeless gesture of placing yourself under the jurisdiction of the Most Holy Trinity – begin by praying the Jesus Prayer with you in the "me" place of the prayer. Then, insert each of your loved ones in turn. ("Lord Jesus Christ, Son of God, have mercy on (*name*), a sinner.") Then and only then, insert the name of the one who you feel has wronged you, hurt you, done damage to you, neglected you. Whatever.

You are thus fulfilling Our Lord's injunction to forgive your "enemy" and, at the same time, shielding yourself from the bitter residue of resentment that can rot your heart and soul.

I'm not joking about this. I know persons who have held grudges, literally, for decades. "Oh I can forgive him/her. But I will never forget." Haven't you heard it before? But that is precisely why Jesus gave us this spiritual "tool" extraordinaire: because we *cannot* forget! That is why we are to forgive "seventy times seven" (*Mt 18:22*). Forget this at your peril. Just pray, even when the old pain wakes you up in the middle of the night; pray for your friends, your enemies. Anyone who the Lord brings to your heart and mind.

You will be amazed at the results – perhaps in them, absolutely in yourself. You may end up making even new friends of old enemies.

Chapter Nine

Offer It Up

At this point in the game, you have realized that the swirling, roiling slop of current events – who is right, who is left, who is winning, who is losing – doesn't give two hoots about a person who has the gift that you have received, the knowledge of mortality that will soon become a reality. In short, the knowledge that "I am going to die soon."

In fact, the noisy parade has passed you by, leaving you sitting on the curb, confetti just stilled at your feet. "Am I worthless?" haunts your mind. "Was all the fussing and hardship, all the attempts to 'get ahead' just an illusion?" To a certain extent, yes. Remember that popular culture does its utmost to keep vast throngs of people from realizing what you now know so well and see so clearly. Ambition – *ambitio* in Latin – means to desire power. For what? Toward what end? So that "the one with the most toys wins?" Were you *that* person? No? Then by those standards, you *are* worthless. The tippy top of the power and glory pyramid allows only one occupant – everyone else is a chump.

But as you know already, since you picked up this book looking for the answer to the Big Question, the world that snatches and grabs in petty meanness what it does not own, the world that hunkers down in bunkers armed with weapons of mass destruction, is filled with delusion, heartache, and failure. You, on the other hand, have received the blessing of knowing what those the poor blighters don't know. And now, amazingly, you are the one who feels sorry for *them*, not yourself.

So the Catholic Church says, this is your opportunity. Use your suffering, your grief, even your demise for the good of those who need it. This is the work of redemptive suffering, and it is called "offering it up."

Archbishop Fulton Sheen once said that when we "assist" at Mass – when we participate in the Holy Sacrifice of the Mass - our suffering, our aloneness, our death, all the things we are going through are united with His Crucifixion and Resurrection in a state of grace that we receive by faith. And if that wasn't enough, Saint Paul reverses the flow, so to speak, and says that *our* suffering, *our* anguish, peril, and, yes, *our* death completes the redemptive work of Our Lord (*Col. 1:23b-24*). By willing to unite our suffering to His in this way we win even more grace.

But wait. Hold the phone. *We* "win" grace? Isn't that why we needed a Savior in the first place – because it is impossible for us to rescue ourselves, let alone "win" any merit alone? God needs *us* to complete the work of salvation?

No. God does not need us to complete the work of salvation. *Without* His grace in Christ's

Death and Resurrection, our lives and deaths would be meaningless, absurd, "a tale told by an idiot, full of sound and fury, signifying nothing," as old Will Shakespeare penned it. But *with* God's grace in His act of salvation, our suffering and death become part of the action; part of His working out the salvation of the world. And the more we willingly "offer up" our sufferings in unity with that of Our Lord, the more grace we receive. It is a matter of intention on our part – do I will that my death become something that Our Lord can and may use?

Just as Our Lady exercised free will (one of the characteristics of being made in God's image), so you can too. We imitate Her beautiful discipleship in *saying Yes* to God in offering up our suffering. This is Marian chivalry, my friend. *Say Yes* like Mary, and see how our travail can help bring salvation into a dark and hurting, foolish and brutal, fearful and hate-filled world.

Pope, Benedict XVI, said it this way: "To pray is not to step outside history and withdraw to our own private corner ... When we pray we properly we undergo a process of inner purification which opens us up to God and thus to our fellow man as well ... We become capable of great hope and thus we become ministers of hope for others. Hope in a Christian sense is always hope for others as well" (*Spe Salvi, 34*).

I recommend the Pope's little book, *Spe Salvi – Saved in Hope –* if you feel led to get it. You yourself must decide how much time you have to spend. He speaks about suffering, Purgatory, letting departed ones know you are praying for them and in turn asking for their prayers, and, of course, hope. If you aren't much of a reader, then I'm deeply honored that you trusted enough to read my book. Reading a lot is fine, but I would rather have you stay close to the Sacraments, your Confessor, and the living Lord in prayer.

What does that look like in terms of "offering it up?" Again, a few suggestions.

I have a good friend who chose to become a Franciscan Tertiary as part of his spiritual discipline to live well and die well. I am a member of *Corpus Christianum*, an association of men and women dedicated to praying for the renewal of Christendom, guided by a Catholic chivalrous spirit and Marian in character.

Most importantly, I recommend using some kind of guide to prayer to order your remaining days and time. If the Liturgy of the Hours is too imposing, try the Little Office of the Blessed Virgin Mary. Pray the Angelus faithfully. Bless your food always. Use an Examination of Conscience before you go to sleep, and commend yourself and those you love to God's care as you do so. Subsume yourself and all egoism to the order of prayer provided in one of many constellations in the Church's galaxy. It will prepare you "further up and further in," as C. S. Lewis said in his Last Battle, for service in God's Kingdom in Eternal life.

Your willingness to *Say Yes* like Our Lady, offering up this reality through which you are traveling is one of the greatest gifts you can give now. And, in my experience, it is one of the greatest joys and consolations of a holy death. After all, remember: there are some really Good Answers to the Big Question. This is one of them.

Chapter Ten

Last Thoughts Before We Go

I need to share one last autobiographical sketch with you. In many ways, I have been blessed to have the chance to rehearse the loneliness and power of death. Before my diagnosis of cancer in my left kidney, I had kidney stones. About twelve, give or take one or two. A friend and colleague of mine had a kidney stone once. She told me that (a) she thought she was dying, and (b) compared to a kidney stone, giving birth to her three children was, and I quote, "a cakewalk."

During my kidney stones moving, scraping, sliding, jerking along from kidney through ureter to bladder, the only thing one can do is drink plenty of water – it pushes them along. But I also found that "offering up" the pain made it possible to "ride" the pain, somehow, since it was not, then, meaningless and random any longer. If there are other world religions or faiths that make suffering as meaningful as the Catholic Church does, I do not know of them.

And that, my friend, is not only a Good Answer to the Big Question. It is very Good News in a landscape made bleak and barren by a fallen race of beings in need of a loving God, a forgiving Savior, and a steadfast and comforting Holy Spirit. One God, Blessed Trinity.

I hope that I've made you smile and think. Maybe you are closer now to answering the Big Question than when you first started reading. Maybe you have even decided to do me one better and write a longer, more helpful book than this "quick read." If I have helped you to open your heart and soul a little more to God and your neighbor in love, I am satisfied.

I'll be praying for you, please pray for me. Life is terminal. You want to make the most of it, even and especially now. Avoid the pitfalls I mentioned, but fly to Confession if you fall in. Serve Our Lord and Our Lady in chivalrous Marian

virtue *saying Yes* as God's grace supports you.
And never stop giving thanks in life and death.
Thank your friends and family, your doctor(s),
any who have prayed for you. You are return-
ing the favor in the work in which you are now
engaged.

I look forward to meeting you and getting to
know you in the future – we'll have all the time
we didn't have in the world. And never forget
Saint Paul's words.

Who shall separate us from the love of Christ?
Shall tribulation or distress, or persecution, or
famine, or nakedness, or peril, or sword? As it
is written,

> *For your sake we are being killed all the day
> long; we are regarded as sheep to be slaughtered.
> (Psalm 44:22)*

No, in all these things we are more than conquerors through him who loved us.

> *For I am sure that neither death, nor life, nor angels, nor principalities, nor things present, nor things to come, nor powers, nor height, nor depth, nor anything else in all creation, will be able to separate us from the love of God in Christ Jesus our Lord. (Romans 8:38-39)*

Jeffry Hendrix

Gaudete Sunday 2008 +

Acknowledgements

and Dedications

To my brother David who beat me to the punch; to my brother-in-arms, Aramis, who taught me how to "do" kidney cancer; to my friend Dawn Eden who pushed me to work on this book almost as much as the Holy Spirit did; to the monks of Holy Cross Abbey, where I received the Sacrament of Confirmation, and whose prayers I fully believe help keep this old world from blowing itself up; to my family of origin who started me on the path to the Catholic Church by teaching me to love God and believe in Jesus Christ as Lord; to all my friends who prayed for me during my bout with cancer; to my sons, Andrew and Maxwell – may the Lord bring them safely one day to Heaven with joy; and to my wife and soul-mate, Mochel, who loved me at my best and at my worst.

Deo gratias. +

Breinigsville, PA USA
03 March 2011
256905BV00002B/12/P